LEAD

Guide a Small Group to Experience Christ

Joel Comiskey

Published by CCS Publishing

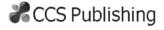CCS Publishing

www.joelcomiskeygroup.com

Published by CCS Publishing
23890 Brittlebush Circle
Moreno Valley, CA 92557 USA
1-888-344-CELL

Third printing, December 2008

Cover design by Josh Talbot
Editing by Scott Boren

All Scripture quotations, unless otherwise indicated, are from the Holy Bible, New International Version, Copyright ©1973, 1978, 1984 by International Bible Society. Used by permission.

CCS Publishing is the book-publishing division of Cell Church Solutions, a resource and coaching ministry dedicated to equipping leaders for cell-based ministry.
Find us on the World Wide Web at **www.joelcomiskeygroup.com**

**Publisher's Cataloging-in-Publication
(Provided by Quality Books, Inc.)**

Comiskey, Joel, 1956-
  Lead: guide a small group to experience Christ / by
Joel Comiskey.
    p. cm.
    Includes bibliographical references and index.
    ISBN 0975581953

    1. Spiritual life--Christianity. 2. Discipling
(Christianity) 3. Group facilitation. 4. Spiritual
formation.   I. Title.

BV4501.3.C6554 2007   248.4
                             QBI06-600333

Table of Contents

Introduction

Leading a cell group is a great way to give to others and receive many benefits in the process. You'll learn how to ask great questions, listen to others, and give pastoral help to the hurting. And as you refresh others, you yourself will be refreshed. As you give to others, you'll receive so much more in return. Just as Jesus said, "Give, and it will be given to you. A good measure, pressed down, shaken together and running over, will be poured into your lap" (Luke 6:38).

You won't be facilitating the group alone because the entire group can help you in the process. Leading a cell group shouldn't be a burden. God has gifted each cell member and the goal is to allow each one to participate as Christ's minister.

If you're working through this book alone, you would benefit from meeting with a coach who can work with you, answer your questions, and hold you accountable. In the appendix, you'll find tips for coaches.

Additional resources

Lead is part of a five-book series to prepare leaders to become mature followers of Jesus Christ. The goal of this book is to teach you to effectively lead a small group.

If you are interested in the other four books in this series, you can purchase them at www.joelcomiskeygroup.com or by calling 1-888-344-CELL. Along with this book, I recommend that you read my books *How to Lead a Great Cell Group* and *Home Cell Group Explosion*. Both of these books can be purchased on the web site or by calling the toll-free number.

You can use this book individually, in a small group setting, or in a classroom. Many churches will teach this material in a group setting. This is the normal way to teach the material, but it's only one way. I've provided teaching outlines and PowerPoints for all five equipping books in this series on a CD. This CD can be purchased at the CCS web site or toll free number.

Understanding the Cell

Biologically, a cell is the smallest structural unit of an organism that is capable of independent functioning. One drop of blood, for instance, has about 300 million red cells! The total genetic package from the parent is re-established in each daughter cell. Blood cells nourish and protect the body by taking nutrients to each body part and then carrying away the waste products. Cells are interdependent with the body and don't function apart from it. Each biological cell grows and reproduces its parts until it divides into two cells. They are constantly dividing to replenish and continue the process.

Just as individual cells join to form the body of a human being, cells in a church form the Body of Christ. They connect people, allow believers to practice the "one-anothers" of Scripture, and make disciples who make other disciples. They also multiply and give life to the entire church.

What is a cell group?

Defining the cell group isn't just an academic exercise. It ensures quality control so that Christ's life continues ministering to each part of the body. Quality must be the guiding principle of any worthwhile definition. The term, "cell group," as used in this book and followed by growing cell churches around the world, is defined as, "a group of 3-15 that meets weekly outside the church building for the purpose of evangelism, community, and spiritual growth, with the goal of multiplication."

You'll notice how this definition gives maximum flexibility yet maintains quality and moves the group forward. Within this definition it's possible to have a wide variety of homogeneity (e.g., a men's cell, family cell, etc.), lesson material, meeting places (e.g., in a house, restaurant, university, etc.) and even degree of participation (some cell groups are directed more by one leader rather than emphasizing participation by all members).

One person said to me that if two people got together once in a while to hammer nails on a roof, he would consider it one of the church's small groups. While this is true in one sense, such a loose definition quickly diminishes quality control. For example, a horseback riding club, a deacon's meeting, or a prison ministry task group are not the equivalent of a multiplying cell group. Granted, each of these groups is small but they do not contain all of the vital, qualitative ingredients set forth in our "cell group" definition. In a deacon's meeting group, for example, it would be very difficult to evangelize (unless the church is quite liberal!). Yet, evangelization is a vital part of the cell.

Try IT!

Read 1 Corinthians 16:19.
Where did the early church meet?

_____

_____

_____

How does today's cell reflect what the early church was practicing back in the first century?

_____

_____

_____

_____

_____

_____

As you prepare to facilitate a cell group or participate on a cell leadership team, I strongly recommend that you maintain a clear definition that should include:

- Small size (cells should remain small enough so that each person can participate and intimacy in relationships can occur).
- Regularity (weekly cell meetings are the norm to assure quality control).
- Penetration (cells meet outside the church building to penetrate the world where people live, move, and breathe).
- Evangelism (evangelism should be prioritized).
- Community (people are dying for relationships and cell groups offer close community. We have been created for community).
- Spiritual growth (cell groups offer pastoral care and spiritual growth for those attending).
- Multiplication (the goal of the cell should be to develop the next leader to continue the process through multiplication).

The goal is to make disciples who in turn produce more disciples. Defining the small group in a qualitative way will ensure that this happens.

Try IT!

How would you define a "cell church" based on your experience?

_____

_____

_____

Why is it important to maintain the quality characteristics of a cell group?

_____

_____

_____

The 4 W's

I don't believe in only one agenda for the cell. There are many great agendas. You'll notice that the order of meeting had nothing to do with my cell definition. I do, however, recommend the 4 Ws (Welcome, Worship, Word, and Witness) as a solid meeting agenda because it allows for maximum participation of group members and is easy to follow.

Each of the 4 W's has a specific purpose. The icebreaker (Welcome) helps people to enter the group dynamic. Prayer and singing (Worship) directs people's attention to the living God. The Bible time (Word) applies God's Word to daily living. Finally, the members are encouraged to share the good news with others (Witness).

Welcome (15 minutes)

The Welcome normally includes some kind of icebreaker. The idea is to connect each person in the group to everyone else. The Welcome time lasts about 15 minutes. Icebreaker questions are varied:

- What do you like to do on vacation?
- What is your favorite hobby?

Try IT!

Do you have a favorite icebreaker? If so, what is it?

_____

_____

If not, make up an icebreaker that you think others would enjoy and use it in your cell group:

_____

_____

_____

_____

Worship (20 minutes)

The Worship time centers on God's worthiness. The cell exists to give glory to God and the Worship time initiates that process. Whether you have a guitar or not, the goal is to give Him glory through worship. You can worship through singing songs, prayer, reading a Psalm, or silence. I encourage everyone to have a song sheet with the songs listed for that evening (normally 5–6 songs on the sheet). Don't worry if no one is present to play guitar or piano. You can always use a worship CD or worship without accompanying music. In between the songs, I encourage the worship leader to allow group members to offer sentence praise, prayer, or silent confession.

Word (40 minutes)

The Word time allows God to speak directly to His people through the Bible. Great leaders draw out others to share their thoughts and apply God's Word. Cell lessons normally have about three to seven questions based on God's Word.

As we'll learn in the next lesson, the best cell leaders are facilitators—not Bible teachers or preachers. I encourage cell leaders not to talk too much because the goal is not information, but transformation. Great leaders help steer the group away from talking about world politics, criticism of the church, or the opinions of different authors. Again, the goal is to apply God's Word to daily living. People should go away changed by God's eternal message.

To begin, I like to ask members to read the Bible verses out loud. I have learned, however, only to ask people to read who I know are confident readers in public. Some like to have the verses printed on a sheet of paper beforehand, using a reader-friendly translation, so that everyone can follow along.

Then I give a brief explanation of the Bible passage. I make sure I don't preach, but members won't know how to answer the questions unless they grasp the meaning of the chapter or verses. I would recommend that the leader take about ten minutes to explain the general Bible passage. A leader doesn't need to be a Bible expert to do this.

Many churches base their cell lessons on the Sunday morning preaching, and thus, cell leaders can take notes while the pastor is preaching the message, knowing that he or she will be covering that topic during cell the following week.

Try IT!

Read James 1:22.
What results in merely listening to the Word?

_____

_____

How does cell ministry help believers to apply God's Word?

_____

_____

_____

_____

_____

Witness (15 minutes)

The Witness time is the last part of the cell group. It focuses on reaching out to others, which may be in the form of planning an evangelistic activity, planning some kind of practical social action ministry, or simply praying in the group for friends and family who need Jesus.

Try IT!

True or false:
☐ The third W means Word.
☐ The fourth W means Witness.

To give you an idea of what a cell lesson might look like, below is a sample cell lesson that I've used on a number of occasions. This sample should give you an idea of the four parts of the cell and how each part flows together.

Sample cell meeting	
Welcome:	• Where did you live between the ages of 7-12? • How many brothers and sisters did you have? • Who was the person you felt closest to?
Worship:	• Read Psalm 8 aloud in unison. • Sing "How Great Thou Art." • Read Psalm 29: let each person read a verse in turn. • Ask for a period of silence for one minute; encourage the members to consider the ways God has comforted them in past situations.
Word:	• Read 2 Corinthians 1:3-5. • Ask, "Share a time when you were in a crisis and God comforted you." • After a time of sharing, then ask, "Can you recall a time when you were used by God to comfort some one else?" • Finally, ask, "Who in our group is in need of God's comfort right now?" • Edify one another as God opens the way to comfort one another.
Witness	• Share names and circumstances of unbelievers who are going through difficult times. • Discuss how we as a cell might witness to these unbelievers by becoming God's agents of comfort in their time of distress.

You can facilitate a cell group

I had the privilege of asking 700 cell leaders in eight different countries to fill out a questionnaire about what made their group grow or not grow. I discovered common factors across all of these cultures. In later lessons, I'll pinpoint areas from the study that had a positive impact on whether or not a cell leader could multiply his or her group. Right now, however, let's focus on factors that had nothing to do with a leader's effectiveness. I think you'll be encouraged. If you want more information about the results of my study, you can purchase *Home Cell Group Explosion* at www.joelcomiskeygroup.com.

Personality

The survey showed that both extroverted and introverted leaders successfully multiply cell groups. Potential cell leaders who tag themselves as "introverts" often say they lack the necessary ingredients to grow a healthy small group. Yet, the survey proved this false. Actually, the introverted cell leader might even be more effective in leading and multiplying a cell because he or she listens more intently. This truth should encourage those who are timid and think they don't have what it takes to facilitate a small group. God will use the personality that He's given you. Psalm 139:13 says, "For you created my inmost being; you knit me together in my mother's womb." Jeremiah 1:5 says "Before I formed you in the womb I knew you, before you were born I set you apart."

Giftedness

Some people think they need to possess a particular gift to effectively facilitate a cell group. The survey showed this wasn't true. It showed no connection between spiritual giftedness and success in multiplication. A cell leader does not need to have one particular area of giftedness to effectively facilitate a cell group.

Successful small group leaders rely on the giftedness of everyone in the cell. Mikel Neumann, professor at Western seminary, authored the book, *Home Groups for Urban Cultures*, in which he discussed the qualities of effective cell leaders. He realized that effective cell leaders were often timid and without any particular spiritual gift. He wrote,

Two people were mentioned to us as productive home group planters. They had started three or more groups, and the leadership seemed a bit puzzled. The woman was exceptionally shy, and the man had trouble expressing himself. I was impressed that it is not outstanding speaking gifts that bring a new home group into existence. Caring and prayer ... are the keys to starting new groups. These leaders allowed other people to participate, recognizing that others had gifts that needed to be used.[1]

---

1. Mikel Neumann, *Home Groups for Urban Cultures* (Pasadena, CA: William Carey Library, 1999), p. 82.

You can be encouraged by the gifts and talents God has given you. You might not feel gifted, talented, or even ready to facilitate a cell group. Remember God is the One who will receive glory in your weaknesses. He'll use the personality and gift mix that He has given you. Paul said in 1 Corinthians 4:7: "For who makes you different from anyone else? What do you have that you did not receive?"

Do IT!
Commit yourself to leading the Word section of your current group to prepare yourself to eventually lead your own group.

Gender
But what about gender? Do male cell leaders do a better job than females? Not at all. The survey showed that females were just as effective in leading and multiplying cell groups as males. God uses both women and men in leading and multiplying cell groups.

Education
Many feel inadequate because they are not well-educated. Yet, education wasn't a factor in determining whether the leader could grow and multiply a cell group. Those with an elementary school education (primary school) were just as effective as those with Ph.D's. The key issue is love and care. Those leaders who loved and prayed for the members could grow and multiply their cell groups.

Memorize IT!
Zechariah 4:6: "'Not by might nor by power, but by my Spirit,' says the LORD Almighty."

What's your excuse?

I want to encourage you. Whether you're male or female, educated or uneducated, married or single, shy or outgoing, a teacher or an evangelist, you can grow your cell group. Later in this book, I will be talking about those factors that are important in leading and multiplying a cell group. Yet, the characteristics covered here (i.e., gender, personality, etc.) are factors you can't change. And they have nothing to do with whether you can lead and multiply a cell group. The factors I'll be covering later are ones that you can change and improve (e.g., prayer, hard work, etc.).

You might feel the weight of your own weakness and wonder how it would be possible to facilitate others in the context of a small group. Yet famous men and women in the past were hampered by incredible limitations as well. Demosthenes, the greatest orator of the ancient world, stuttered! The first time he tried to make a public speech, he was laughed off the rostrum. Julius Caesar was an epileptic. Beethoven was deaf, as was Thomas Edison. Charles Dickens was lame; so was Handel. Homer was blind; Plato was a hunchback. Sir Walter Scott was paralyzed.

The common thread with these people is that they each refused to rely on the common excuses for failure. They turned their stumbling blocks into stepping stones. God will use who you are to minister to many people. Trust in Him and watch Him do great things through you.

Try IT!

What are some of the excuses that you've used or heard others use for not being able to facilitate a small group?

_____

_____

_____

_____

_____

_____

Do those reasons still hold true after completing this lesson? Why or why not?

_____

_____

_____

_____

_____

_____

_____

_____

_____

Remember IT!

What stood out to you in this lesson?

_____

_____

_____

_____

Main points:
1. A great cell definition includes seven components: small (3–15), weekly, outside the church building (to penetrate into the community), evangelistic, intimate community, spiritual growth (discipleship), and multiplication.
2. The small group order called the 4 Ws includes: Welcome (15 minutes), Worship (20 minutes), Word (40 minutes), and Witness (15 minutes). Flexibility is important and following the Spirit of God is essential.
3. Anyone can successfully facilitate a small group. It doesn't depend on personality, giftedness, education, or gender. What's most important is a willingness to allow God to use you.

Apply IT!

1. Memorize the seven parts of the cell group definition. Share those seven parts with someone else without referring to your notes.
2. Write down the fears you have about your own personal ability to lead a cell group and compare those with your new understaning about cell leadership.

Facilitating the Group

"**L**et my people go."

God spoke these famous words through Moses to Pharaoh when he refused to obey God. God continues to speak these words to Christians today. Sadly, many believers are trapped in the pews of the church. They come on Sunday, hear a sermon, and go home. The professional minister does all the ministering while the Christian sits, listens, and observes. Yet, the Bible says that we are all ministers, and that God has called us to serve. According to Ephesians 4:11–12, the work of pastors and ministers is to equip and prepare the members to do the work of the ministry.

As you learn how to facilitate a cell group, you'll be the minister. But just remember that your goal is not simply to get people to come and listen to you. Your job is to empower others and to help them to minister. By all means, don't fall into the trap of dominating those in the group. Your role is to empower them.

People come to the group because they have personal needs and want a chance to share those needs. Allow them to share and grow.

Ask stimulating questions

Silence. Jim's attempt to stimulate discussion failed. "Is there anyone else who'd like to comment on this verse?" Still no response. Jim decided it was best to break the silence by launching into a spontaneous sermon of the Bible passages. "At least they're receiving God's Word," he assured himself.

I know how this leader felt. I've faced similar periods of strained silence as I've lead the lessons in my own small group. Often the problem has to do with dull, boring questions. Closed questions, for example, have one correct answer. When a leader uses too many of them, he positions himself as the Bible expert who's trying to discover the brightest, most Biblically literate students. Few people respond to this type of question.

Open-ended questions, on the other hand, elicit discussion and sharing. This allows for more than one right answer to be offered. Open-ended questions stir cell members to apply the Biblical truths to their own lives.

An example of a closed-ended question is, "Where did God want Jonah to preach?" There is one right answer—the city of Nineveh. An open-ended question is: What is an example in your own life when you felt God was telling you to do something (like Jonah) and you hesitated?

Questions that Grab the Heart	
Examples of questions that generate discussion:	Example of closed questions that elicit one answer:
<ul><li>How do you feel about. . . ?</li><li>Share your experience concerning. . .</li><li>Why do you feel this way?</li><li>How would you ... ?</li></ul>	<ul><li>Do you agree with this passage?</li><li>What is the first book of the Bible? .</li></ul>

Cell questions, whether open-ended or closed questions, come in three varieties: observation, interpretation and application.

Observation	Interpretation	Application
Understanding what the Bible passage says.	*Clarifying what the Bible passage means.*	*Putting the Bible passage into practice in our everyday lives.*

An observation question is simply observing what the text says. It's asking the question, "What does this passage say?" Take John 3:16. An observation question from this verse might be, "How did God demonstrate his love for us?" You'll notice that the answer lies within the text: "God so loved the world that he gave his one and only Son." Interpretation goes one step further. Interpretation asks the question: "What does this verse or passage mean?" John 3:16 says, "God so loved the world." An interpretation question is: What does the word world mean? Is John talking about the planet? The people on the planet? A worldly system apart from God?

But while observation and interpretation are both important in understanding God's Word, the goal of the cell group is application. To apply John 3:16, for example, you could ask the question, "How has God shown His love to you?" or "When was the first time you experienced God's love?" Each person could contribute something.

Try IT!

Write down your own observation question from John 3:16:

_____

_____

_____

Write down your own interpretation question from John 3:16:

_____

_____

_____

Write down your own application question from John 3:16:

_____

_____

_____

In the cell group, I recommend a general principle of one application question for every two observation questions. You won't need to use many interpretation questions—if any.

The example on the next page will give you an idea of observation and application questions. These questions come from a cell lesson I prepared from Psalm 90.

1. Read Psalm 90:9–10. How does the Psalmist describe the condition of man? *(observation question)*
2. Share an experience when you realized how short life really is (e.g., the death of a parent, car accident, near death experience, etc.) *(application question)*
3. Read Psalm 90:4–6. How does the Psalmist describe the way we should view our time? *(observation question)*
4. Describe your feeling when you think about eternity (e.g., fear, confidence, joy). Why do you feel this way? *(application question)*
5. Share a fear that you have of the future (at the end of the cell, pray for one another) *(application question)*
6. Read Psalm 90:12. What does Moses want God to teach him? *(observation question)*
7. In your opinion, what does the phrase, "count our days" mean? *(interpretation question)*
8. What are some concrete actions that you can take this week to live in the light of eternity? *(application question)*

You'll notice that I started some of the questions above with share rather than the normal who, what, why, etc. I call this an "exhortation question." The word share reminds the group that the cell discussion is not an "exam" and that comments are welcomed. Opened-ended questions grab the heart and generally elicit more than one response.

Observation questions are more focused on what the Bible actually says. And since we want to base the study on God's Word, these questions are very important. Open-ended application questions, however, should be a vital part of the study. People must go away transformed.

Do IT!
Read Philippians 4:13. Prepare a cell lesson of 5-7 questions with at least two open-ended application questions. Ask a cell leader or supervisor to review it (and be ready to use your lesson in a cell group).

Let others share

I've been to cell groups in which the leader wanted to dominate everything. In one group I visited, the leader clung to the mini-service mentality. He cut short the icebreaker to get into the "study" quickly.

With a Bible in one hand and a document that looked like a manuscript in the other, the leader proceeded to dominate the meeting for the next 40 minutes. My spirit grieved for those who were forced to sit through another service. He answered his own questions and even controlled the concluding prayer time.

This leader, like many, was so comfortable in hearing his own voice that he kept on talking and talking. Avoid the mini-service syndrome.

Try IT!

Read Proverbs 18:13.
How does the writer describe someone who doesn't listen well?

_____

_____

_____

On a scale of 1–10, how would you describe your listening skills at this moment? What do you need to do to improve?

_____

_____

_____

Effective leaders, on the other hand, concentrate on the contributions of others through attentive listening. Careful listening is love visibly expressed to group members. The best cell leaders are more concerned about what other people are saying than their own lesson. I remember one cell meeting in which the cell leader would ask a question, and then shuffle through his notes in preparation for the next question, while the person was answering the first question. The people got the impression that what they had to say really wasn't very important. The cell group is all about the people present. It's not about you. Listen attentively and people will be glad they came.

Create responsiveness

I believe it's very important to respond positively to someone's answer, even if it's not correct. You want to encourage the person, rather than making him or her feel foolish because the answer wasn't exactly right. You are rewarding involvement, not correctness. Responding positively makes the person feel like the contribution is truly important. Judy Hamlin says, "Never totally reject any idea. Try to isolate the negative and explore the good in the idea. Affirm the idea-giver, even though you might not fully agree with the idea. Don't ever tell someone they are stupid. If you do, trust will be totally destroyed and no one else will speak." You might say, "That's interesting. What do the rest of you think?"[2] No one wants to hear that they are stupid.

Granted, someone might state an opinion contrary to God's Word. Yet, even in those moments, the cell leader can begin with, "Thanks for sharing your opinion. Now let's look at what God's Word says about this." Or if the cell leader knows that mature believers are present, he or she might say, "What do the rest of you think?" or "Nancy, what do you think about this issue?" Whenever addressing participants, use their names with a warm and positive tone in your voice.

Because approximately 70 percent of all communication involves body language, it's important to watch your gestures and those of others in the group. Non-verbal actions, such as a bored look, an incredulous stare, or a humorous glance to a friend, express what a person is actually thinking. If you look at your watch while someone else is talking, what does that say to the person? Or if you tap on the ground in an obvious show of discomfort, do you think they'll feel like you've truly listened to them? No.

Give people time to think

After asking a question, the leader should give the group time to think. People need to sort through a number of possibilities to determine

---

2. Judy Hamlin, *The Small Group Leaders Training Course* (Colorado Springs, CO: Navpress, 1990), p.115.

Try IT!

Read Ephesians 4:29.
What kind of words should come out of our mouths?

_____

_____

_____

How can you apply this verse in your own life? How should you respond to cell members during the lesson?

_____

_____

_____

what they're going to say. The leader has looked at the questions. The members have not. They are hearing the question for the first time. Each member is not only trying to interpret the question, but also trying to figure out other group dynamics (e.g., who will speak first, etc.).

Sadly, many leaders don't recognize this natural process and when there's not an immediate response, the leader jumps in and starts teaching or preaching. Don't fear silence in the group. The fact is that cell leaders tend to fear silence more than the cell members do. Give others a chance to answer.

Another error is thinking the question has been fully answered after one person responds. Unless it's simply a yes or no type question, people can respond in more than one way. God has made each person different with a unique perspective on life. The response of Jane, for example, might be exactly what Mary needs to hear. If you move on too quickly, that response won't happen. Also remember that some people get warmed up slower than others. A cell leader should not move on too quickly.

> ## Memorize IT!
> **James 1:19: "My dear brothers, take note of this: Everyone should be quick to listen, slow to speak and slow to become angry."**

Effective leaders facilitate others

Synonyms for facilitate are "to assist," "to aid," "to empower," and "to make easy." Great leaders empower others to shine. As we've already seen, effective cell leaders help others by asking questions, attentive listening, and stimulating others to respond. An effective small group leader clarifies and restates ideas, stimulates discussion, cares for people, is enthusiastic, practices transparency, listens intently, explains clearly, helps people share their feelings, is open to varied opinions and evaluations, and can summarize thoughts and draw conclusions.

> ## Try IT!
> Check the boxes that you need to work on:
> ☐ Clarifies and restates ideas
> ☐ Can get everyone to talk
> ☐ Demonstrates care for others
> ☐ Is enthusiastic
> ☐ Practices self-disclosure (being vulnerable)
> ☐ Asks stimulating questions
> ☐ Listens intently
> ☐ Explains clearly
> ☐ Helps people share their true feelings
> ☐ Is open to varied opinions and evaluations
> ☐ Can summarize thoughts and draw conclusions

Tips in dealing with talkative people

If you have a talker in your group, I recommend one or more of the following tips to deal with him or her:

- Sit next to the talker in order to give less eye contact. Sitting next to the person and avoiding eye contact will signal that you're not encouraging him or her.

- Call on other people to give their opinions. By calling on individuals by name, you're assuming leadership responsibility and directing the conversation of the group.
- Redirect the conversation away from the talker, if he or she pauses.
- Talk directly with the person. Talking directly with the person, after or before the cell group meeting will often solve the problem.
- Ask the person to help you make the meeting more participatory. When the talker understands the larger reason for the cell group and even how to participate in fulfilling this goal, it's likely the person will change.
- Clarify the rule that no one is allowed to speak a second time until everyone has had a chance to speak for the first time. It will remind the talkers in a clear, concrete way to remain quiet until others have shared.

Try IT!

Which of the above suggestions for silencing the talker do you like best? Why?

_____

_____

_____

_____

_____

_____

_____

_____

Remember IT!

Which scripture verse quoted in this lesson impressed you the most?

_____

_____

_____

_____

_____

_____

Main points:

1. Small group leaders are not called to "preach" but to facilitate the cell.
2. Effective facilitation takes place as the leader listens well.
3. The leader should respond positively to each member.

Apply IT!

1. Pick any passage of Scripture. Write two observation questions and two application questions.
2. Next time your group meets, make it a point to listen attentively to each answer.

Ministering to People

The night that Michael came to the cell group, he seemed normal. After the lesson on forgiveness from 1 Peter 4:8, however, his need became clear. He shared his deep resentment toward the person who had raped his daughter years earlier. Michael had been clinging to his bitterness and it had left him joyless and enslaved. That night the Word of God reached deep into his soul, and Michael realized he needed to be set free. During the prayer time, Michael confessed his bitterness, and the group members prayed for him to experience healing.

Michael needed healing and reconstruction in his life. And ultimately that's what the cell group is all about. If people go away touched and ministered to, you've had a successful cell group. If that doesn't happen—even though everyone sang on key, the icebreaker was fun, and people responded well to the questions—the group missed the mark.

The word edification literally means "to build or construct." Paul wrote to the Corinthian church, "What then shall we say, brothers? When you come together, everyone has a hymn, or a word of instruction, a revelation, a tongue or an interpretation. All of these must be done for the strengthening [edifying] of the church" (1 Corinthians 14:26).

People in our society often appear happy, but inwardly they're crying out with multiple emotional wounds. It doesn't take long to notice that people are outwardly suffering the symptoms of inner wounds. Proverbs 15:13 says, "A happy heart makes the face cheerful, but heartache crushes the spirit."

The crushed spirit that characterizes so many is the result of childhood abuse, divorced parents, unforgiveness, resentment, destructive habits of a parent, rejection, depression, guilt and various types of fear.

People need a Savior to touch them and work healing in their hearts. Only God can heal and set people free. God is vitally concerned with changing people's lives. He says in Isaiah 63:9: "In all their distress he too was distressed, and the angel of his presence saved them. In his love and mercy he redeemed them; he lifted them up and carried them all the days of old." God is distressed by the people's hurts, fears, and doubts. He wants to use your cell group to bring healing.

I believe the cell is the best atmosphere for people's lives to be reconstructed and for them to grow in the grace and knowledge of Jesus Christ. In the small group, the Holy Spirit, the Master Craftsman, challenges and changes people. The intimate atmosphere of the small group makes it possible for this edification to take place.

Try IT!

Think about a cell meeting when people were built up. What happened to open the door for such ministry?

_____

_____

_____

_____

_____

_____

_____

_____

_____

_____

Allow the Holy Spirit to guide you

The most important thing the leader can do is hear the voice of God and then minister accordingly. What is Jesus saying? Try to spend time with God before the cell meeting starts. Allow God's Spirit to fill you until you sense His fullness of joy and exceedingly great riches. Allow Him to infiltrate your mind, your attitude and your emotions. Psalm 16:11 declares: "You have made known to me the path of life; you will fill me with joy in your presence, with eternal pleasures at your right hand."

More than lesson preparation, small-group success depends on the leader's personal spiritual preparation. Remember that He wants to speak through you. Be available and willing to be used by Him— obeying whatever He reveals. Become a channel of the Holy Spirit. Allow Him to guide and direct.

Try IT!

Read 1 Thessalonians 5:11.
How does Paul say we should respond to each other?

_____

_____

_____

What can you do to build someone up in your group?

_____

_____

_____

_____

_____

_____

Minister to anyone who shows up

It doesn't matter if only one or two people show up—as long as they go away edified. I've noticed, in fact, that when the group is smaller, more people have a chance to share personally and receive God's touch.

One evening Monica arrived early to our cell group, she began to pour out her heart: "I'm so thankful I'm no longer living with Andy. I feel clean inside, but it's still so hard; at times, I feel like I need him." Frank and Kathy arrived in the middle of our conversation and began to minister to Monica from their own experience. My wife also spoke words of encouragement to her, and eventually all of us began to pray for Monica. My wife and Kathy understood Monica's needs more deeply than I, and their prayers hit the emotional nerve center of what Monica was going through. No one else came to the cell that night and the five of us saw God's power at work transforming her life.

Sometimes cell leaders don't feel "successful" unless a large group shows up. Yet, when the goal is the reconstruction of people's lives, the cell leader will be ready to minister even if only one or two arrive.

Get others involved in the edification process

Each member of Christ's body can minister healing to others. No one should sit on the sidelines. Miracles often occur when every member becomes a minister, and they begin to see themselves as instruments of healing. Larry Crabb, famous author and psychologist, wrote:

Ordinary people have the power to change other people's lives. The power is found in connection, that profound meeting when the truest part of one soul meets the emptiest recesses in another. ... When that happens, the giver is left more full than before and the receiver less terrified, eventually eager, to experience even deeper, more mutual connection.[1]

---

1. **Larry Crabb**, *Connecting* (Nashville, Tenn.: Word Publishing, 1997), 31.

Try IT!

Read 1 Corinthians 14:12.
How should the gifts of the Spirit be practiced?

_____

_____

_____

How can you use the gifts and talents God has given you to build others up?

_____

_____

_____

_____

The power of small-group ministry is discovered by allowing each member to minister and connect to each other. I attended one cell meeting in which the leader asked members to pick their favorite songs during the worship time. After each song, the cell leader asked the person to explain why he or she picked that particular song. One lady, Theresa, picked a song about renewal, and later began to sob. "I had an angry confrontation with my husband today. I discovered he's seeing another woman," she blurted out. "I feel so dirty. Please pray for me." Everyone in the group laid their hands on Theresa and prayed for her. The group spent the time necessary to meet her need. She had come to the meeting bruised and beaten down, but she left filled and encouraged.

The standard for success in small-group ministry is whether the members leave the group edified—whether healing took place in people's lives—not whether a particular order or plan was followed.

Instruct the group to listen to needs

It's best for the cell leader to advise the group to listen, rather than quickly responding with pat answers to people's problems. When someone is facing a crisis, it's not the moment to say, "You just need to trust in the Lord. Don't you know that all things work together for good to those who love God, to those who are called according to His purpose?"

This advice, while 100 percent correct, will actually do more harm than good to a hurting, grieving person. Before becoming ready to hear advice, the person first must know that God's people will help bear the burden. He or she is longing for a listening ear—not a quick response of an often-quoted scripture passage. Healing takes place in the silence of skilled listening and love. God is the sensitive Healer, and He desires that His people listen to others.

Listening is so powerful. It works wonders because it causes people to feel special, loved, and cared for. When someone shares an important need, we must allow God to flow in a very special way and manifest Himself. Just be quiet. Be silent before God, and allow Jesus to minister to that person's needs.

After the burden is shared, there should be a moment of silent understanding. As group members empathize with the person, godly counsel will ensue: "Joan, I can relate to your fears and doubts brought on by your friend's cancer. When my brother faced brain cancer, I felt those same fears. I wrestled for days, wondering why God would allow this disease to strike my family. But then God showed me . . ."

Encouragement brings healing

I remember being in one small group in which the leader offered a slight criticism to every response. "You almost have it," James would say. When another person responded to the answer, James retorted, "No, that's not it, but you're getting closer." The dance to find the right answer continued. *This is like a high-school quiz,* I thought to myself. As James reached the last few questions, the participation ground to a screeching halt. No one wanted to risk embarrassment. The fear of failure permeated the room.

The best small-group leaders view themselves as God's healing agents and encourage all to participate; knowing that encouragement is one of the primary ways to minister God's healing touch. They practice the words of Proverbs: "Pleasant words are a honeycomb, sweet to the soul and healing to the bones" (16:24). Great small-group facilitators guard against any information or comments that are not edifying—that destroy rather than build up.

Like Christ, the small-group leader should gravitate to those with needs in the group, offering Christ's healing power to the hurting. The leader must boldly proclaim Christ's desire to heal today—physically, spiritually, and emotionally. The hospital nature of the cell group is a truism that we must accept: God's healing power is made manifest in the sweet atmosphere of the cell.

Try IT!

Read Hebrews 10:24–25.
What's a key reason for meeting together according to these verses?

_____

_____

What can you do this week to encourage others during the cell meeting?

_____

_____

_____

_____

_____

_____

Develop transparency in the cell

People's lives are transformed when they are honest with each other. When people hide behind walls of superficiality, little is accomplished. Effective cell leaders encourage people to share honestly and openly about anything and everything.

Try IT!

Read 1 John 1:7.
What happens when we walk in the light?

_____

_____

_____

How does this verse apply to transparent sharing in the cell group?

_____

_____

_____

_____

The leader must model transparent sharing if he expects others to follow. Group members will typically be as transparent and open as the leader is willing to be. If the leader isn't willing to risk transparency and openness, the members will certainly not step out. If the leader always wants to give the best impression, the other cell members will do likewise.

Some leaders imagine that they're promoting transparency, but their testimonies don't resonate with the members. "Pray for me," they might say. "I became slightly impatient with a fellow worker today. That's the first time I've ever had a conflict at work. Please pray." Testimonies like this close people off, causing them to think the leader is a super-saint, when in fact, that's not the case.

Try IT!

Is it difficult for you to share transparently? Why or why not?

_____

_____

_____

_____

_____

_____

Transparency is also the best evangelistic tool to reach non-Christians. People without Christ appreciate authenticity. They're thankful when Christians share struggles, because often the non-Christian is going through situations far worse, but without Jesus to help. Cell evangelism through transparency is a very natural activity, and it penetrates the defenses of those who would never darken the door of a church building, but who need love and a sense of belonging.

Even if you don't have a major problem to share, you can still talk about the small, daily difficulties you face. We all struggle with long waits in line, unwanted calls, computer breakdowns, demanding work schedules and other irritations of life. Transparent sharing, however, doesn't only involve sharing difficulties. What about your desires and plans? Transparency means talking about yourself in an honest way, allowing others to know your strengths, weaknesses, aspirations, dreams and hopes.

> **Memorize IT!**
> **Romans 15:1-2: "We who are strong ought to bear with the failings of the weak and not to please ourselves. Each of us should please his neighbor for his good, to build him up."**

Edification often happens outside the cell

Not all community or ministry happens in the cell group. Cells are often the springboard for one-on-one relationships that take place outside the meetings. Janet, a member of our cell group, silently suffered in her marriage because of a total blackout of communication. She wisely didn't blurt out the hurt she carried (which would have maligned her husband to those in the group). She did, however, spend hours with my wife outside the cell meeting, receiving prayer and encouragement. God ministered to her in the small-group environment but healed her in the relationships that extended from the cell.

Effective cell groups develop close bonds. They do more than a meeting. The close bonds they develop within the cell stirs them to spend time together outside the cell meeting. As a leader, encourage such activity and even plan outside meetings (outside activities, camping, sporting events, etc.).

Remember the cell leader doesn't have to do everything. I encourage cell leaders to tell members to minister to one another. I received an email from a pastor I'm coaching that said, "One thing that came up during our discussion was the problem of time. Several of the leaders were wrestling with guilt over not being able to spend time with their cell folks apart from the meeting and celebration." My response was, "One important truth is that the cell leader should not feel like he or she needs to develop all the relationships. ... Cell members are equally responsible—in fact, perhaps more so, because they don't have the additional job of leading." Ecclesiastes 4:9–12 says, "Two are better than one, because they have a good return for their work: If one falls down, his friend can help him up. But pity the man who falls and has no one to help him up! Also, if two lie down together, they will keep warm. But how can one keep warm alone? Though one may be overpowered, two can defend themselves. A cord of three strands is not quickly broken."

Do IT!

Make it a point this week to encourage someone--specifically someone who is discouraged and would be helped by your encouragement.

Remember IT!

What is one thing from this lesson you want to share with someone close to you?

_____

_____

_____

_____

_____

_____

Main points:
  1. Edification literally means "to build up."
  2. Edification is the key or guiding essence of the cell. The leader can measure the success of a cell meeting by whether people went away edified.
  3. Each member should be an instrument of edification.

Apply IT!

1. Think of someone you can build up in the cell. Make plans to build that person up through listening, prayer, using your gift, etc.
2. Prepare to share a transparent area of your life in the cell meeting. This might be a positive or negative aspect of your life.

Creating a Spiritual Atmosphere

Vince Lombardi, a famous National Football League coach, turned the losing Green Bay Packers into a championship team. Under Lombardi's direction, the Packers collected six division titles, five NFL championships, two Super Bowls (I and II) and acquired a record of 98–30–4. Once, after losing a game, he called for a team meeting in the locker room. As he faced these seasoned, hardened men who knew the game of football inside and out, he held up a football and announced, "Men, this is a football!" He then began to remind them of some of the fundamentals of the game and said, "Men, we must get back to the basics." Lombardi knew the importance of never forgetting the basics— the fundamentals of the game. He believed that the strength of their game lay in the foundations of football—the very basics.

The "basics" of a God-honoring cell group is Christ in the center. The number one thing that a cell facilitator can do to place Christ in the center is to make sure he or she is spiritually prepared before the cell group starts. It's a mistake, in fact, to think that anything is more important than the leader's spiritual preparation before the group starts (such as refreshments, lessons, a vacuumed rug, etc.). Remember the story of Mary and Martha— Christ's positive response to Mary demonstrated that the most important item on our agendas is time spent with Him. Basking in God's presence will fill you with the power, insight and confidence necessary to successfully lead your group to new heights.

Successful cell leaders pray

In lesson one, I talked about how effective cell leadership had little to do with outward leadership characteristics such as personality, gender, gifting, or education. Yet, one characteristic that strongly correlated was the leader's prayer life. The statistical study showed a relationship between time spent with God and whether or not the leader multiplied his or her cell group.

The cell leaders surveyed were asked: "How much time do you spend in daily devotions? (e.g., prayer, Bible reading, etc.)." They chose one of five options, ranging from 0 to 15 minutes daily to over 90 minutes. The following table summarizes the devotional patterns of those cell leaders who filled out a questionnaire:

Devotional Patterns of Cell Leaders	
0 to 15 minutes	11.7%
15 to 30 minutes	33.2%
30 to 60 minutes	33.8%
60 to 90 minutes	7.6%
90 minutes +	13.7%

In this same questionnaire of 700 cell leaders, the leaders were asked whether their group had multiplied and, if so, how many times. Those who spent 90 minutes or more in daily devotions multiplied their groups twice as much as those who spent less than half an hour.

During quiet times alone with the living God, the cell leader hears God's voice and receives His guidance. In those still moments, the leader understands how to deal with the constant talker, how to wait for a reply to a question, or how to minister to a hurting member of the group. Cell leaders moving under God's guidance have a keen sense of direction and leadership. Group members respond to a leader who hears from God and knows the way. God brings success. This statistical study is simply further proof of that.

A leader first learns about personal guidance for his own life. Then, as he or she demonstrates that guidance, the leader can shift to determining how and where God is leading the group. A leader who repeatedly demonstrates that God speaks to him gains spiritual authority.

Daily devotional time is the single most important discipline in the Christian life. During that daily time, Jesus transforms us, feeds us, and gives us new revelation. On the other hand, not spending sufficient time with God can bring the agony of defeat. How often have we raced out of the house, hoping to accomplish a little bit more, only to return bruised, depressed, and hurt? When we start the day without time with our Lord, we lack power and joy to face the demands of life.

And didn't Jesus say the same thing when he said, "But when you pray, go into your room, close the door and pray to your Father, who is unseen. Then your Father, who sees what is done in secret, will reward you" (Matthew 6:5–6).

The statistical study also showed that not only does the leader's devotional life determine whether or not the cell multiplies, but the cell leader's prayer for cell members determines whether or not the cell is effective in multiplication. When comparing prayer, contacting, and social meetings, it was discovered that prayer for group members is the leader's most important work to unify and strengthen the group in preparation for multiplication. A cell leader can increase his or her effectiveness by praying daily for the cell members.

Try IT!

Read Hebrews 11:6.
How will God respond to those who diligently seek Him?

_____

_____

_____

How can you apply this verse in your own life this week?

_____

_____

_____

_____

_____

_____

One practical thing that the cell leader can do is spend time praying before the cell begins. This gives the cell leader new power because the Spirit of God works in him or her. Remember that effective cell leadership is all about God's work. It's all about allowing the Spirit of God to move, bless, and anoint.

Effective cell leaders highlight the anointing of the Spirit over information, and obedience over knowledge. Leadership effectiveness depends on the Spirit giving guidance and ultimate victory. The Spirit will work and He'll guide.

We must remember that the Spirit wants to fill us. He's willing. Some people think that it's so hard to be filled with the Spirit—as if we had to work for it. No. The Spirit is here now. He wants to fill us. He is able to fill us. Our need is to receive His great blessing.

Try IT!

How important is prayer in your own life right now?

_____

_____

_____

_____

_____

_____

Commit yourself to making prayer your top priority.

The Spirit empowers through weakness

One lesson I've learned about the Holy Spirit is that He doesn't want our self-sufficiency. He receives the most glory when He's in control, not us. When we're the weakest, He's the strongest. Often in those very moments when we feel the most frail, disoriented and unsettled, the Holy Spirit has the greatest opportunity to manifest His strength, power and creativity. The Holy Spirit longs for us to cling and cry out to Him.

When we're strong, we don't usually feel the need or desire to do so. But our helplessness creates the opportunity for us to jump into His arms. Throughout the Old and New Testaments, we see a God who searches for vessels that will look to Him and give Him glory. God had to take away the fighting forces of Gideon, for example, so that he would not boast in his own strength. When God whittled Gideon's army down to 300 men and the chances of human victory were virtually impossible, God told Gideon to go ahead. And as always, God came through in a miraculous way (Judges 7).

God gave Paul a "thorn in the flesh"—a painful trial—so that Paul would keep his eyes on God alone. Even though Paul pleaded with God to remove the trial, God refused, saying, "My grace is sufficient for you, for my power is made perfect in weakness" (2 Corinthians 12:9). Paul concluded, "Therefore I will boast all the more gladly about my weaknesses, so that Christ's power may rest on me. That is why, for Christ's sake, I delight in weaknesses, in insults, in hardships, in persecutions, in difficulties. For when I am weak, then I am strong" (2 Corinthians 12:9–10).

Paul wrote that God has chosen people who are weak, foolish and despised in the world's eyes, so that His glory would be acutely manifested and everyone around would immediately recognize the grace and power of God. It's clear throughout Scripture that God wants all the glory (1 Corinthians 1:31).

If you as a small-group facilitator feel weak and inadequate, you're in the right place! Your weakness is the Holy Spirit's opportunity to glorify the Father. Rather than plead with God to remove your insecurity, ask God to receive glory through it. God loves to use weak small-group leaders who look to Him rather than to themselves.

One of my heroes is a woman named Lorgia Haro. Back in 1995, Lorgia hesitated to even host a small group. The leader of the group she attended was moving, and I practically pleaded for someone to host the group while we searched for another leader. Lorgia hesitantly raised her hand, but she shared her own feelings of inadequacy due to her timid nature and the fact that her husband was not a Christian.

Try IT!

Read 2 Corinthians 12:10.
Think of three areas where you feel "weak" with regard to facilitating a cell group:

_____

_____

_____

_____

_____

_____

Now meditate on how God can receive glory through each of those areas of weakness. Begin to rejoice in God's power in your weakness.

Lorgia fulfilled her commitment and opened her house. Unlike Lorgia, we didn't fulfill our commitment—we never did find a leader for that group! In the absence of anyone else to lead the group, Lorgia stepped up to the plate. She asked for the Holy Spirit's strength before each meeting. Her shyness forced her to depend on God's strength, and through her weakness, Jesus used her to love people into the kingdom. The group grew. As she grew in confidence of the Holy Spirit's power, she encouraged members to facilitate their own groups. "If I can do it," she reasoned, "you can, too!" Within the space of seven years, her group multiplied twelve times and more than 70 people received Christ. Her husband was one of those converts. Our church grew tremendously because of one weak, shy woman named Lorgia Haro.

Keep your focus on His power in your weakness. Jesus wants to be strong through you. You're nothing apart from Him. Keep your eyes on His power.

Using spiritual gifts in the cell

The Holy Spirit gives spiritual gifts to each of His children. 1 Peter 4:10 says: "Each one should use whatever gift he has received to serve others, faithfully administering God's grace in its various forms." Each of us has at least one gift. And the best place to discover spiritual giftedness is in the small group atmosphere.

Try IT!

Read Ephesians 4:16.
What is Paul talking about here when he uses the word "ligaments"?

_____

_____

_____

How can the cell group enhance each person functioning as part of the body?

_____

_____

_____

_____

_____

_____

_____

Do IT!
Determine what you think your main spiritual gift is. Ask someone in the group this week if he or she thinks that you have that particular gift (i.e., believes that you have effectively exercised that gift)

I tell people trying to identify spiritual giftedness to determine their desire level. Exercising a gift should not be a chore. Rather, it should be enjoyed. Do you like explaining biblical truth? Perhaps you have the gift of teaching. Do you enjoy praying for people in the group and see them healed? Perhaps you have the gift of healing. Do you love to bring refreshments and help out? Perhaps you have the gift of helps. Are you drawn to visit cell members who are having problems? Perhaps you have the gift of mercy.

Another key test is confirmation from others. I tell people to look for affirmation from those in the group. If you have a particular gift, others will benefit from your use of the gift. In the relational context of the cell group, each person has a chance to use his or her gift and receive feedback. Do people notice your capacity to clarify the meaning of Scripture? If so, you probably have the gift of teaching. Do people come to you after the cell for counsel? My wife's gift of counseling (exhortation) has been confirmed over and over in the small-group environment. Again, the best place to discover your spiritual gift is in the context of relationships, and the cell group provides an ideal "relational" atmosphere .

Memorize IT!
1 Corinthians 14:1: "Follow the way of love and eagerly desire spiritual gifts, especially the gift of prophecy."

Try IT!

Read Romans 12:3–8.
Why does Paul say that we shouldn't think too highly of ourselves?

_____

_____

From the various gifts listed, which one (s) do you believe God has given you?

_____

_____

_____

_____

_____

No one particular gift is needed in cell leadership

Successful cell leaders don't solely depend on their own gifts: They rely on the Holy Spirit's power to marshal the gifts of everyone in the small group. Great cell leaders truly see themselves as facilitators of others. They don't try to do everything themselves. They don't wear the "super-leader" shirt. The best small-group leaders, in fact, get out of the way and allow energized small-group members to lead the way.

I have concluded that successfully facilitating a small group is related more to the spiritual maturing process of a believer than what gift the leader possesses (or doesn't possess). Nothing matures a believer more than depending on God to prepare a lesson, facilitate the small group, care for the members and motivate the group to reach non-believers. The Holy Spirit uses the process of small-group facilitation to grow and mature the leader, and I'm convinced that anyone can successfully facilitate a small group, although not everyone will do so.

Additional Resources on Spiritual Gifts	
Scripture passages:	I Corinthians 12, Romans 12, and Ephesians 4.
Books on spiritual gifts:	My favorite book is Peter Wagner's *Discovering Your Spiritual Gift* (Ventura, CA: Regal Books, 2005). Christian A. Schwarz's, *The 3 Colors of Ministry* (St. Charles, IL: ChurchSmart Resources, 2001) is my second favorite. My book *The Spirit-filled Small Group* goes into detail about spiritual gifts and small groups (Grand Rapids, MI: Chosen Books, 2005). This book can be purchased at www.joelcomiskeygroup.com.
Spiritual Gift Tests:	Dr. Mel Carbonell's gift survey offers a gift inventory and the DISC personality evaluation. Contact: 1-800-501-0490 or www.uniquelyyou.com (published by Uniquely You, Inc.). Also available is Alvin J. VanderGriend's gift survey (developed and published by the Christian Reformed Church, CRC Publications). Contact: 1-800-4-JUDSON; Paul Ford's gift survey (published by ChurchSmart Resources)is available by contacting 1-800-253-4276.

Remember IT!

What portion of this lesson had the most impact on you?

_____

_____

_____

_____

_____

Main points:
1. Prayer should permeate the small group.
2. Effective cell leaders focus on praying.
3. God has at least one spiritual gift for you, and the best place to discover it is the context of the cell.

Apply IT!

1. During the next cell meeting, have a prayer time after the cell lesson. Ask the men to go to one room and the women into another to share more in-depth prayer requests.
2. Determine what spiritual gift God has given you by asking yourself what you like to do and asking others what they think you're good at.

Multiplying Cells

E ach of us began as a single cell. This cell couldn't move, think, see, or do things like laugh and talk. But the one thing it could do, and do very well, was divide—and divide it did. The lone cell became two, and then four, then eight and so on, in time it became the amazing person that you are today. Think of how far you've come. And it all started in a single cell! Cells are the smallest form of life—the functional and structural units of all living things. Your body contains trillions of cells, organized into more than 200 major types. One of the key cell functions is multiplication (or "division" in biological terms).

Some people think that talk of multiplication is just another way of referring to statistics and numbers. In reality, just the opposite is true. Cell multiplication equals cell health. Healthy cells are multiplying cells. Weak cells, on the other hand, focus on themselves, never reach out, and ultimately become ingrown. The reason the cell has to focus on evangelism and leadership development is to remain healthy.

The constant danger of the small group is to become fat and sassy. Members imagine that seeing the same people week after week will maintain the community but ultimately it kills it. Cells need fresh nutrients to survive. Thus, when visitors enter and a new cell leader is raised up to multiply into another cell, group health is maintained.

Christian Schwarz spearheaded a research project called Natural Church Development. The research center in Germany now has more than 20 million pieces of data about why churches grow and don't grow. Schwarz discovered that multiplication was one of the key health factors in growing congregations. Schwarz says," If we were to identify any one principle as the most important, then without a doubt it would be the multiplication of small groups."[1]

Try IT!

Read John 16:21–22.
How does Jesus describe giving birth?

_____

_____

_____

What is the long-lasting result of giving birth, according to Christ?

_____

_____

_____

_____

Giving community to others

How can new people come into the group and the group still maintain a deep level of community? This is a common objection to cell evangelism and multiplication. Research and experience show, however, that better, more biblical community develops when a cell reaches out to non-Christians. The newer person actually adds to the growth of the believers in the group by giving them an opportunity to minister—and thus grow.

---

1. Christian A. Schwarz, *Natural Church Growth* (Carol Stream, IL: ChurchSmart Resources, 1996) p. 32.

When a small group has a common evangelistic objective, it starts working together to accomplish a goal. The common objective creates a unity and camaraderie. Everyone gets involved—from the person who invites the guests, to the one who provides refreshments, to the one who leads the discussion. The team plans, strategizes, and finds new contacts together. Eventually it multiplies and continues the process.

The friendship and love (community) develops in the process of reaching out to non-Chrstians as a group. Today's broken society desperately needs a loving family. The cry of the lost drives cells to share their rich community rather than hoarding it among themselves. When multiplication takes place, new groups are available for lost people to receive wholeness.

Try IT!

Read Acts 13:2–3.
What did the Holy Spirit say to those fasting and praying?

_____

_____

To what extent has the Holy Spirit been involved in preparing and sending off the new leader or leadership team from your cell? What can you do to emphasize God's work in multiplication?

_____

_____

_____

_____

_____

_____

Try IT!

True or false:

☐ Every one loves to multiply groups.

☐ People don't often realize that multiplication is a health issue.

☐ Only very talented people can multiply groups.

Evangelism and intimacy = multiplication

Bigger is not better for small groups. Cells must remain small to maintain unity. After a certain number, there's no longer the opportunity for shy Mary to express herself. Why? Because she doesn't like to talk in large groups. She's only willing when there are a small number of people.

Most small group experts say that the maximum size for a group is between 12–15 adults. It may get a bit larger with kids (although in most family cells, the children break off during the Word time and go to another room in the house to have their own lesson). The reason to keep the group small is to maintain intimacy.

Thus, in reality, to maintain the small size of the group but to continue to reach out to new people, each group has to think seriously about raising up a new leader or leaders and multiplying into a new group. The other alternative is not to invite anyone new and maintain a small size. But remaining small without evangelizing doesn't coincide with the great commission, in which Jesus told us to make disciples of all nations (Matthew 28:18–20).

Do IT!

Share with someone in the group (or the entire group) why multiplication is necessary to keep the group healthy, rather than being a statistical "numbers" thing. Prepare your heart to participate in cell multiplication.

Doing a lot of things right

To multiply a cell group, you as the leader must do a lot of things right. Many people equate cell multiplication with evangelism, but evangelism is only part of the equation. Cell multiplication involves evangelism, visitation, study, leadership training, small group dynamics, discipleship, and pastoring. If the leader only focuses on discipleship, the group will grow inward and stagnate; if the leader solely concentrates on small group dynamics, leadership development will suffer; if the leader only focuses on evangelism, many will slip out the back door.

Cell multiplication embraces so many other leadership qualities that it deserves the central focus of cell ministry. Yet in reality, multiplication equals leadership development. I've noticed that some churches allow the same leader to facilitate two or more cell groups. I think it's wise to say one leader per cell—and in fact, it's best to have a leadership team in each cell.

Some churches allow the cells to become so large that only "super pastor" types can lead them. I believe that anyone can successfully lead a small cell group of three to fifteen people. Leadership for larger groups, however, require an additional set of skills, gifts, and talents.

Memorize IT!
John 15:8: "This is to my Father's glory, that you bear much fruit, showing yourselves to be my disciples."

How to multiply a cell group

The traditional way of multiplying a cell group is called mother-daughter multiplication. The group grows to approximately fifteen people, and then six to eight people start the new cell. This has worked effectively for many churches and is a great way to go because the new group starts strong. The leader or team of leaders in the new group has gone through the training track and is ready to guide the new group.

When using the mother-daughter process of multiplication, the cell group goes through the process of *learning* about each other and determining who is committed to the group. This might last for a couple months. Then there's the *loving* stage. Those who are committed decide to love in spite of the problems. The *linking* stage is when the core of the cell is firmly developed and truly linked together. The *launching* time period is when the group is ready for action and is reaching out effectively. Finally the *leaving* step is when the multiplication actually takes place.

Another effective way to lead a cell group to multiplication is to encourage each member of the cell to go through the training track. The first one to finish the training can take one or two people from the mother cell group and plant a new cell. This is called "cell planting." Cell planting doesn't wait for a certain number of attendees in the cell to plant another one. One type of cell planting occurs when the cell leader goes off to plant his or her own cell, and leaves the original cell with one of the members who has completed the equipping process (I personally prefer this method).

Try IT!

Read Genesis 1:28.
What is God's desire for mankind?

_____

_____

_____

Do you believe that Jesus desires multiplication for the cell group? Why or why not?

_____

_____

_____

_____

_____

_____

_____

I was once in a church in which the leader felt that none of the members were competent to lead a cell group. "They all seem dysfunctional," she confided with me. During that week she heard me talk about raising up lay people to do the work of the ministry, and she became excited about the possibilities. She decided to replace herself in the original cell group while she planted another one. When she left, the group came alive under the new leader!! She was the one having problems!

I used to place exact time frames on when a cell should multiply. I no longer do this. I've discovered that it all depends on the receptivity of the people. In places like Bogota, Colombia, the time it takes to multiply a cell is about six months, but in places like Zurich, Switzerland it might take two years. The difference? Receptivity to the gospel and willingness of the people to become disciples.

Try IT!

Read Ecclesiastes 4:12.
What is the main point of this verse?

_____

_____

_____

How can this verse apply to cell multiplication?

_____

_____

_____

_____

_____

_____

_____

Remember IT!

Which scripture verse quoted in this lesson impressed you the most?
Why?

_____

_____

_____

_____

_____

_____

Main points:
1. Group fellowship or community is a byproduct of cell evangelism and multiplication.
2. Cells must remain small to maintain intimacy but must evangelize to fulfill the great commission. The only alternative is to raise up new leaders and multiply.
3. Mother-daughter multiplication takes place when the cell reaches a certain size and half the group leaves to start a new group. Cell planting doesn't depend on how many are in the mother cell and only requires a new leader to launch a new cell.

Apply IT!

1. On a scale of 1–10, would your small group be more in-reach oriented or outreach oriented (1 being in-reach and 10 being outreach)?
2. In the cell group, share what you've learned about how small groups must remain small but continue to reach out. Encourage those in the group to consider multiplication.

Working Diligently

I n 1996, I visited a cell group at Bethany World Prayer Center that was about to give birth. All of the staff was present to celebrate this wonderful occasion. The cell leader sat proudly in one corner and I could tell he was enjoying the attention. We celebrated that night with gumbo and barbeque—a true feast. Afterward, when all had departed and the cell leader was alone in the room, I asked him, "What is the secret to your success? What did you do that brought you to this place?" His answer was frank. "For months our group plodded along without any fruit. I considered giving up," he confessed. "Yet, by the grace of God, I continued doing the things that I knew I should do. I kept praying, inviting, and making contact. Then suddenly a young person came to the cell, received Jesus, and began to invite his friends. Now here we are ready to multiply!"

Plodding. Some believe that you have to be at the right place at the right time and that luck governs all of life. The cell leader at Bethany came to believe that it wasn't about being in the right place at the right time but about pressing ahead and not giving up!

Basketball legend, Larry Bird, excelled at shooting free throws by practicing 500 shots each morning before school. Demosthenes of ancient Greece became a great orator by reciting verses with pebbles in his mouth and speaking over the roar of the waves at the seashore.

Successful cell leaders keep on doing the things they know they should do. With practice, their leadership is perfected. They are willing to do what it takes to make their cells successful.

In the next lesson, I will discuss some of the factors that can affect multiplication in a positive way (e.g., time spent outside the cell meeting, setting clear goals, visiting the cell members, etc.). The common thread behind all of those factors is the word "diligence." God must ultimately convert souls and change lives. Yet, God uses diligent workers who press on in the face of obstacles.

Diligence characterizes effective disciple-makers

The Greek word for diligence is the word "spoudé." What does this word mean? According to the Greek lexicon, this word means quick movement in the interests of a person or a cause, to hasten oneself, speed in carrying out a matter, to give yourself trouble. It refers to a person who is active, industrious, zealous, and takes great pains to do his work. This word stands in contrast to laziness. In fact, Paul tells us that we must be diligent in our leadership, dedicated wholeheartedly to our work. "If it is encouraging, let him encourage; if it is contributing to the needs of others, let him give generously; *if it is leadership, let him govern diligently*; if it is showing mercy, let him do it cheerfully" (Romans 12:8).

Try IT!

Read Proverbs 13:4.
What happens to the diligent? The sluggard?

_____

_____

_____

How can you apply this in your daily life?

_____

_____

_____

_____

There is an old saying: "Champions don't become champions in the ring—they are merely recognized there." It is diligent, secret training before the fight begins that propels a boxer to win. 2 Timothy 2:15 says, "Do your best (spoudé) to present yourself to God as one approved, a workman who does not need to be ashamed and who correctly handles the word of truth."

Try IT!

Read 2 Peter 3:12–14.
Why are the readers exhorted to "make every effort"? (the three words used in English equals the one word spoudé)

_____

_____

_____

What is one area in which you can practice diligence this week?

_____

_____

_____

_____

_____

_____

_____

What do you see?

Most of us have heard about the two shoe salesmen who went to a jungle tribe. Both noticed that few people wore shoes. One wired back to the home office, "Our company has no future here. There is no market for our product. No one wears shoes." Another salesman fired off a wire with a markedly different message: "We have a gold mine of a market here. Everyone needs shoes!" Do you only see giants—or do you see the giants and God's power to overcome them?

Try IT!

Read Mark 11:22–23.
What does Jesus tell us about faith?

_____

_____

_____

What is it that you need to believe God to do in your life?

_____

_____

_____

_____

_____

_____

_____

_____

I've noticed that some cell leaders are always making excuses. They only see the problems and the potential pitfalls. When talking about raising up new disciples, they make a million excuses. Others press on in the face of opposition and do great things for God.

Try IT!

True or false:

☐ Talented people always succeed over those who have less talent.

☐ Spoudé can be practiced by anyone

☐ Some are gifted with the ability to work hard.

I remember Paul. He had lost a job building gasoline stations and didn't have transportation to come to my house. I decided to pick him up—he along with all his family members. Every Thursday night, the entire clan would come to my house for our cell meeting, then I would drive them home in my car. As you can imagine, after a long day of work, I didn't feel like taking them home. But the good news is that on the way home every Thursday, I had the chance to disciple Paul. Eventually Paul became a cell leader and even multiplied his cell (I became a grandparent!).

Memorize IT!
Proverbs 14:23: "All hard work brings a profit, but mere talk leads only to poverty."

Don't give up

John Maxwell says, "Perhaps the most valuable result of all education is the ability to make yourself do the thing you have to do, when it ought to be done, whether you like it or not; it is the first lesson that ought to be learned." We're all filled with worthy intentions, but few actually live out their intentions. Effective leaders translate intention into reality. Perhaps this is the one thing that great leaders do best—they press ahead when others give up. Are you willing to do that? Abraham Lincoln is a great example of diligence (spoudé):

• In 1832, he lost the election to become a state legislator

- In 1833, his personal business failed.
- In 1835, his sweetheart died.
- In 1836, he had a nervous break-down.
- In 1838, he was defeated in his race for Illinois House of Representatives.
- In 1843, he lost the election to Congress.
- In 1848, he lost the congressional election for the second time.
- In 1849, he was rejected for land officer.
- In 1854, he was defeated in the election to become a U.S. senator for the third time.
- In 1856, he lost the election for vice-president of the U.S.
- In 1858, he once again lost for senator.
- In 1860— after 28 years of failure—he won the U.S. presidency.

Abe Lincoln wasn't deterred by his failures. He allowed his failures to create in him strength of character and the fortitude to press on. He remained diligent in the face of obstacles and difficulties. His character remained firm throughout.

Do IT!
Think of an area where you've been discouraged in cell ministry. Determine to press on in that particular area in spite of the odds and obstacles.

Spoudé reminds us to press on when we feel like giving up. It's not going to be easy. Thomas Edison once said that genius is 99% perspiration and 1% inspiration. I like to say that the best small group leaders know how to sweat. They know how to work hard. They press on until it works; they don't give up easily. The founder of Honda Motors, Soichiro Honda, said, "Many people dream of success. To me success can only be achieved through repeated failure and introspection. In fact, success represents the 1 percent of your work which results only from the 99 percent that is called failure." According to Soichiro, the reason we don't succeed is because we haven't learned to fail. We so easily give up in the battle. We work when we feel like it and when we don't feel like it, we quit.

Try IT!

Read Proverbs 14:23.
What is the result of all hard work? Mere talk?

_____

_____

On a scale of 1–10, if hard work was 10 and mere talk was 1, where would you place yourself? Why?

_____

_____

_____

_____

_____

Nike's slogan "just do it" summarizes the theme of spoudé. Don't sit around and talk about it. Just do it. Don't think, think, and think some more about it. Be proactive and just do it. Some people are so filled with good intentions and great thoughts that they never do anything.

Let me be clear: I am not saying that hard work should only be directed to leading a cell. I believe, in fact, that the number one area where we need to work hard is in our relationship with God and our family. True success, I believe, is having the love and respect of your closest family and friends. Thus, if you're a successful cell leader and a failure at home, you need to change your priorities. My point is that too often we tend to make excuses instead of pressing ahead. I believe we too often give up when success is right around the corner.

Remember IT!

Write out a prayer right now asking God to help you understand and apply one thing from this lesson.

_____

_____

_____

_____

_____

_____

Main points:
1. The word in the Greek for diligence is spoudé.
2. Hard work is the key ingredient behind successful cell multiplication.
3. Those factors that affect multiplication are within the leader's control.

Apply IT!

1. In what specific area of cell leadership do you need to be more diligent?
2. Apply yourself in that particular area to be more diligent in the following week.

Working Smart

Michael Jordan was the greatest basketball player of all time. Few dispute this fact. Yet, when Jordan first joined the Chicago Bulls in 1984, he realized that he had to make major improvements to win a championship. Phil Jackson, his coach during most of his playing years, wrote, "When he first came into the league in 1984, he was primarily a penetrator. His outside shooting wasn't up to professional standards. So he put in his gym time in the off-season, shooting hundreds of shots each day. Eventually, he became a deadly three-point shooter." Jordan also improved his team play and by 1988, he was averaging eight rebounds and eight assists each game—along with his thirty-three point average. Jordan's ability to focus and make needed adjustments eventually helped the Chicago Bulls win three consecutive national championships between 1991–1993.

Likewise, you as a cell leader need to know how to focus—how to work smart and not just hard. You need to know how to channel your diligence to guide the group forward. My research confirmed that certain practices definitely helped multiply cells.

In the first lesson of this book, I talked about what cell leaders don't need to do in order to multiply their cell groups. They don't need a certain personality type, spiritual gift, level of education or gender. While prayer is the most important characteristic that is needed, the survey also showed that the actions set out below also correlate positively with cell multiplication.

Encourage relationships among members

Effective leaders encourage relationships among members apart from the cell meeting. The leader knows that the cell meeting is only one aspect of cell life. As we discussed in a previous section, relationships between cell members are just as needed—if not more necessary—outside of the cell group.

The leader might encourage group members to meet together before work to pray and keep each other accountable. Hebrews 3:12–13 says, "See to it, brothers, that none of you has a sinful, unbelieving heart that turns away from the living God. But encourage one another daily, as long as it is called Today, so that none of you may be hardened by sin's deceitfulness."

Some cell leaders have felt overwhelmed by trying to do everything. I remind leaders that they don't have to develop all the relationships. I stress to leaders the need to stimulate the members to meet with each other.

Relationship building events include picnics, meals, sports events, or even going on camping trips. Some of these events will be the actual cell meeting, but often such events are extra-curricular, either among people from the group or the cell itself.

Try IT!

Additional group activities
- ☐ Car wash
- ☐ Barbeque
- ☐ Yard sale
- ☐ Concert

What would you add?

_____

_____

_____

_____

_____

_____

Reach out and attract visitors

Some leaders just expect people to show up at the cell meetings. The effective ones, however, mobilize the cell to reach out and bring new people into the group. Rather than hindering the cell, great leaders know that visitors bring fresh life to the cell group.

When Leo's son showed up at the cell group, we were thrilled. That same night, Adrienne's brother and son also visited. The cell came alive. We sensed a new vigor and purpose in the cell group. Everyone wanted to minister and reach out.

Try IT!

Read John 4:39–42.
What did the Samaritan woman do as a result of her encounter with Christ?

_____

_____

_____

How have people been influenced by your testimony? Give examples

_____

_____

_____

_____

_____

_____

_____

Something exciting takes place when visitors come. They make the community new and fresh. The cell can give away its gift of community to a hurt and dying world that knows nothing of Christ-like fellowship. The church becomes the church to others.

Wise cell leaders don't take it upon themselves to do all the inviting. They are constantly encouraging the group to help in the process. The survey revealed that cell leaders who weekly encourage members to invite visitors double their capacity to multiply their groups—as opposed to those leaders who do so only occasionally or not at all. Cell leaders might conclude the meeting by setting forth the vision for outreach in the cell. "Michael, who are you going to invite next week?" Michael might say, "My cousin Tim." The cell leader could respond, "Oh that's great. Let's pray that your cousin Tim will respond favorably to your invitation."

Set cell multiplication goals

My survey showed that those cell leaders who knew the date for cell multiplication were far more likely to actually multiply their cell than those who failed to set a goal. Goals simply give direction to the group.

When my wife was pregnant with Sarah, our first child, everything revolved around planning for that special day. We had to find a crib, clothes, prepare the room, and especially practice for the delivery. I like to tell cell groups that they are already pregnant ... now plan for the delivery. The difference is that multiplication might take longer than nine months. Yet, try to envision the when, who, and where as best as you can. Remind the group why multiplication is necessary. Frame the vision in terms of fulfilling the great commission of Jesus—raising up disciples who will lead the new cell.

David Cho, the founder and pastor of the largest church in the history of Christianity, said, "Many people criticized me because I was giving goals to my people then encouraging them to accomplish the goals. But if you don't give them a goal, they will have no purpose for being in the cell ... If they have no goal, then the people will gather together and just have a grand fellowship." It seems that Cho was giving his people multiplication goals. If the cell leader along with the cell comes up with the goal, it's even better.

Try IT!

Read Joshua 14:6–15.
How did Caleb include God in his goal? (verse 14)

_____

_____

Using the example of Caleb, describe your goal for cell group multiplication.

_____

_____

_____

_____

_____

One important reason why goal setting is necessary is because cell groups have the tendency to turn inward and to become self-absorbing. Cells need a clear cut goal to keep them outwardly focused. Human biological cells possess a genetic code that tells them to divide into two cells. It's part of their genetic composition. When a cell leader instills the goal of multiplication, it's like setting the genetic code to give birth in the group.

Try IT!

True or false:
- ☐ A cell multiplication goal gives direction to the group.
- ☐ Cell multiplication goals should be rigidly kept, even though the mother group dies in the process.
- ☐ A multiplication goal keeps the group focused outwardly.

Memorize IT!
Proverbs 15:22: "Plans fail for lack of counsel, but with many advisers they succeed."

Make contact

The survey showed that cell leaders who maintained contact with those who attended the cell were far more effective in preserving the unity and guiding the group toward multiplication. Whether visiting cell members or newcomers, it's important to maintain contact. The verse in Proverbs comes to mind, "Be sure you know the condition of your flocks, give careful attention to your herds" (Proverbs 27:23). A visitation or a call can really make a person feel wanted and cared for. Such an act of kindness will also encourage the person to come back.

Granted it can be a chore to make contact. Picking up the phone can seem like lifting a heavy weight because so many things compete for our attention. In such moments, remember Nike's slogan, "Just do it." I remember one missionary told me, "I don't have the gift of making phone calls." I wanted to say, "Just do it!"

Do IT!
Make contact this week with someone from your cell group that needs you (telephone or personal visitation). Pray with the person.

Often people will show up in the cell group and only talk in generalities. They don't really share much of who they are, and so it's hard to get to know them in the cell meeting. When I've taken the time to go out for coffee and get to know the cell members as individuals, I've formed bonds of relationships that have lasted.

Try IT!

From what we've covered thus far in this lesson, check the disciplines below in which you are the weakest. Then circle the ones in which you are the strongest:

☐ Encouraging relationships among members.
☐ Reaching out and attracting visitors.
☐ Setting goals for multiplication.
☐ Making contact with members and visitors from the cell.

The cell leader need not make all the contact. Ask a committed core member, for example, to visit new members or someone who hasn't shown up for quite some time (you will need to follow-up to make sure the contact took place). Once again, the issue is sharing the responsibility. You don't have to do everything yourself.

Remember IT!
What had the most impact for you in this lesson?

_____

_____

_____

_____

_____

_____

_____

_____

Main points:

1. Along with prayer, certain tasks help the leader multiply his or her cell.

2. The four areas covered in this lesson are: encouraging relationships among members, reaching out and attracting visitors, setting a date for multiplication, and making contact with those in the cell groups (members and visitors).

Apply IT!

1. Talk with key people in your group about a goal date for multiplication. After praying about it and setting the date, make an announcement in the cell.

2. Plan a social activity with your cell to increase intimacy among members.

Making Disciple-makers

John Wesley and George Whitefield were famous preachers. Each lived during the 18th century and belonged to the same holy club at Oxford University. Both desired to win a lost world for Jesus Christ and were eager to try new methods to do so. In fact, George Whitefield preached in the open air before John Wesley. Most believe that George Whitefield was a better preacher than Wesley. Benjamin Franklin once calculated that Whitefield could easily preach to a crowd of 30,000 people (without a microphone). Whitefield probably even recorded more decisions than Wesley because of the huge crowds he attracted.

Yet, there were some major differences between the two as well. At the end of his life, George Whitefield said this, "My brother Wesley acted wisely. The souls that were awakened under his ministry he joined in classes [cell groups], and thus preserved the fruits of his labor. This I neglected, and my people are a rope of sand."

Christ knew that in order to transform the world, He would need to concentrate on specific people. Jesus didn't neglect the multitude, but He focused on His disciples, who provided supervision and discipleship to the rest. Mark 9:30–31 tells us, "Jesus did not want anyone to know where they were, because He was teaching His disciples." Christ left the crowds in order to concentrate His energies on His disciples, who would eventually lead the Church.

Lack of harvest workers

Scripture says, "When he [Jesus] saw the crowds, he had compassion on them, because they were harassed and helpless, like sheep without a shepherd. Then he said to his disciples, "The harvest is plentiful but the workers are few. Ask the Lord of the harvest, therefore, to send out workers into his harvest field. He called his twelve disciples to him and gave them authority to drive out evil spirits and to heal every disease and sickness" (Matthew 9:36–10:1). Jesus is concerned about those who don't know Him today! They are just as lost today as they were back in Bible times. One of the best ways to reach people is to get them involved in a cell group and prepare them as laborers for the harvest.

Try IT!

Read Matthew 28:18–20.
What does Christ command his disciples to do?

_____

_____

How does raising up leaders in cell ministry apply to Christ's Words?

_____

_____

_____

_____

_____

_____

_____

_____

_____

Apprenticing future leaders

Some people think that only certain people can be ministers. They think that only those with a degree or extra training can be a cell leader. Yet, Revelation 1:6 tells us, "To him who loves us and has freed us from our sins by his blood, and has made us to be a kingdom and priests to serve his God and Father." You are a minister. You are a priest. You are called to minister to others.

Begin now to see others as disciple-makers. The most important job of a cell leader is not to find members to fill the group but to develop the next disciple who will make more disciples. Actually, one of the main reasons for the cell is to develop disciple-makers. A disciple-maker is one who is facilitating a cell group and raising up new leaders within to eventually multiply. This is the process. In other words, cells are "leader breeders."

This means that we have to continue to disciple others to expand the number of future leaders in God's kingdom. And this is what cell ministry is all about. It's raising up an army of future leaders.

God has called us to apprentice future leaders. This is a biblical way of life. Moses tutored Joshua and Elijah trained Elisha. The apostles were recruited and trained by Jesus. Barnabas discipled Paul, who in turn developed Timothy. Can you point to someone who you are developing?

Do IT!
Take the next step to become a cell leader. If you're already a cell leader, approach someone in your group about taking the next step to become a cell leader (disciple-maker).

The goal of the cell group

The goal is to transform each cell member into a disciple who makes other disciples. Each person in the cell should receive training and prepare to facilitate a cell group or form part of a future team that leads a group.

You might have heard the story of Michelangelo who passed by a huge chunk of marble that lay by the roadside. Another sculptor had become discouraged with the marble and discarded it. Michelangelo began to stare at that chunk of marble. He continued to stare until one of his friends became impatient and said, "What are you staring at?" Michelangelo looked up and said, "I'm staring at an angel." He could see something wonderful and worthwhile in a broken piece of stone.

Each person that walks into the cell group must be seen as a potential angel. What you want to see in people is a desire to grow, dependence on God, a servant attitude, and willingness to serve. Remember that you're not looking for outstanding gifts and talents.

Try IT!

Read 2 Timothy 2:1–3.
What is Paul's main point to Timothy in this passage?

_____

_____

_____

Do you see yourself developing a disciple? Why or why not?

_____

_____

_____

_____

_____

_____

_____

_____

Try IT!

What have you been doing to raise up new leadership in your cell group?

_____

_____

_____

_____

In what specific area do you need to focus your effort?

_____

_____

_____

_____

_____

_____

_____

Risking for Jesus

Sometimes we have the tendency to criticize Peter, when in fact Peter had the courage and faith to step out of the boat! "'Lord, if it's you,' Peter said, 'tell me to come to you on the water.' 'Come,' he said. Then Peter got down out of the boat, walked on the water and came toward Jesus" (Mt. 14:27–32).

Those who risk for Jesus always have the possibility of stumbling and falling. But it's in that process that we learn valuable lessons. If we never step out, we do little for Jesus. Remember, the goal of the cell leader is to help each cell member step out of the boat.

Try IT!

On a scale of 1–10, how would your rate yourself as a risk-taker?

_____

_____

With regard to cell leadership, what is the next step you need to take? Make concrete plans to take that step:

_____

_____

_____

_____

_____

_____

_____

_____

_____

_____

_____

James Kouzes and Barry Posner say, "Leaders venture out. Those who lead others to greatness seek and accept challenge. Leaders are pioneers—people who are willing to step out into the unknown. They're willing to take risks, to innovate and experiment in order to find new and better ways of doing things."[1]

Memorize IT!
Matthew 9: 37–38: "Then he said to his disciples, 'The harvest is plentiful but the workers are few. Ask the Lord of the harvest, therefore, to send out workers into his harvest field.'"

Two fundamentals

The first fundamental is to allow each cell member to perform one of the significant cell tasks (e.g., lead ice-breaker, worship, prayer, lesson, and evangelism time). Apprentice cell leaders need to practice "stepping out of the boat." Potential cell leaders will learn the most when they are actually involved.

My counsel is to provide an experience; get feedback; review the feedback with the apprentice cell leader; probe for principles learned; provide another experience, and continue in this fashion.

The second fundamental is to make sure the potential cell leader receives training. The cell leader doesn't have to do all the training, but the cell leader makes sure that the training actually takes place.

Use titles with great caution. People like to have a title. But often, once they have the title, they're content with a particular role and never move beyond that point. I think it's better to call each person a potential cell leader. Some will get there before others, and that's fine.

---

1 James M. Kouzes & Barry Z. Posner, *The Leadership Challenge: How to Keep Getting Extraordinary Things Done in Organizations* (San Francisco, CA: Jossey-Bass Publishers, 1995), pp. 9-10.

Remember IT!

What had the most impact for you in this lesson?

_____

_____

_____

_____

_____

_____

_____

Main points:
1. The Bible says that each person is a minister. No one is called to sit in the boat!
2. Christ's solution to win the world is to raise up harvest workers from the harvest.
3. Apprenticing future leaders is a Biblical way of life.

Apply IT!

1. Interview a cell leader who has multiplied his or her cell group. Write down the principles of cell multiplication that you discover.
2. Meditate on the fact that every person can be a disciple maker. Plan specific steps to use each cell member in some aspect of the cell.

How to Coach Someone Using this Material

Many churches will teach this material in a group setting. This is the normal way to use the material, but it's not the only way. If you choose to teach a group of people, outlines and PowerPoints are provided for all five equipping books on a CD. You may purchase this CD at www.joelcomiskeygroup.com or by calling 1-888-344-CELL.

Another way to train someone is to allow the person to complete each lesson individually and then ask someone of the same gender to coach him or her. The coach would hold the "trainee" responsible to complete the lesson and share what he or she is learning.

I believe in multiple methods for teaching material. The fact is that not everyone can attend group-training meetings. But the person still needs training. Coaching is a great option.

Coaching the trainee through the material

Ideally, the coach will meet with the trainee after each lesson. At times, however, the trainee will complete more than one lesson and the coach will combine those lessons when they meet together.

The coach is a person who has already gone through the material and is now helping someone else in the training process. Additionally a coach must have:

- **a** close walk with Jesus.
- a willing, helpful spirit. The coach doesn't need to be a "teacher." The book itself is the teacher—the coach simply holds the trainee accountable with asking questions and prayerful encouragement.

I recommend my book, *How to be a Great Cell Group Coach*, for additional understanding of the coaching process (this book can also be purchased on the CCS web site or by calling 1-888-344 CELL). The principles in *How to be a Great Cell Group Coach* apply not only to coaching cell leaders but also to coaching a trainee. I recommend the following principles:

- Receive from God. The coach must receive illumination from Jesus through prayer so he has something of value to give to the trainee.
- Listen to the person. The coach's job is to listen to the trainee's answers. The coach should also listen to the trainee's joys, struggles, and prayer concerns.
- Encourage the trainee. Often the best thing the coach can do is point out areas of strength. I tell coaches to be a fanatic for encouragement. We all know our failures and have far too much condemnation hanging over us. Encouragement will help the trainee press on and look forward to each lesson. Try to start each lesson by pointing out something positive about the person or about what he or she is doing.
- Care for the person. The person might be struggling with something above and beyond the lesson. The material might bring out that specific problematic area. The best coaches are willing to touch those areas of deep need through prayer and counsel. And it's one hundred percent acceptable for the coach to simply say, "I don't have an answer for your dilemma right now, but I know someone who does." The coach can then go to his or her own coach to find the answer and bring it back the next week.
- Develop/train the person. Hopefully the person has already read the lesson. The goal of the coach is to facilitate the learning process by asking specific questions about the lesson.
- Strategize with the trainee. The coach's job is to hold the trainee accountable to complete the next lesson and/or finish the current one. The coach's main role is to help the trainee sustain the pace and get the most out of the material.
- Challenge the person. Some think that caring is good but confronting is wrong. The word care-fronting combines the two

and is what the Bible promotes. If we truly care, we'll confront. The Spirit might show you areas in the trainee's life that need to come under the Lordship of Christ. The best approach is to ask for permission. You might say, "Tom, may I have permission to speak to you about something I'm noticing?" After the person gives you permission, you can then tell him what the Lord is laying on your heart.

First session

When the coach meets with the trainee, the Holy Spirit will guide the session. Creativity and flexibility should reign. I do recommend, however, the following principles:

• Get to know the person. A great way to start is to use the Quaker questions. This will help you to warm up to each other. After the first week, the coach can open in prayer and simply ask about the trainee's life (e.g., family, work, studies, spiritual growth, etc.)

Quaker questions
1. Where did you live between the ages of 7–12?
2. How many brothers and sisters did you have?
3. What form of transportation did your family use?
4. Whom did you feel closest to during those years?

• Be transparent. Since you've already completed this training material, share your experiences with the trainee. Transparency goes a long way. Great coaches share both victories and struggles.

"Coaching questions" to use each week

A great coach asks lots of questions and listens intently. The goal is to draw the answers from the trainee so that he or she applies the material to daily living. Key questions to ask each time are:
1. What did you like best about the lesson(s)?
2. What did you like least about the lesson(s)?
3. What did you not understand?

4. What did you learn about God that you didn't know previously?
5. What do you personally need to do about it?

The coach doesn't have to ask each of the above questions, but it is good to get into a pattern, so the trainee knows what to expect each week.

Pattern to follow each week
1. Prepare yourself spiritually before the session begins.
2. Read the lesson in advance, remembering the thoughts and questions you had when you went through the material.
3. Start the session in prayer.
4. Ask the coaching questions.
5. Trust the Holy Spirit to mold and shape the trainee.
6. Close in prayer.

Index

A

Abraham Lincoln, 65
agenda, 10
Application, 20
atmosphere of the cell, 35

B

Baptism, 3
Beethoven, 16
Bethany World Prayer Center, 61
Bible, 2, 87
body language, 24
build up, 35, 39

C

Caesar, 16
cell church, 9
cell lesson, 12
cell meeting, 13, 23, 30, 31, 33, 35,
    38, 39, 51, 61, 62, 65, 69, 70
cell planting, 57
Chicago Bulls, 69
Christ, 87
Christian Schwarz, 53
close bonds, 38
Closed questions, 19

Coaching, 85, 87
Community, 9
concentrate, 23, 77

D

David Cho, 72
Demosthenes, 16, 61
devotional time, 42, 61
diligence, 62
discipleship, 9, 18, 57, 77

E

edifying, 29, 35
Edison, 16
Education, 15
Encouragement, 34, 86
encouragement, 86
Evangelism, 9, 9, 56, 56
extroverted, 14

F

facilitator, 41, 45
forgiveness, , 29

Breinigsville, PA USA
07 September 2010
244940BV00003B/2/P